Sweet Treats

Gourmet Eats

Chef Firecracker

H4TS Publishing books may be purchased for educational, business, or
sales promotional use. For information, please write VP of Events,
H4TS Media, LLC at info@h4tsmediallc.org or
6025 Surrey Square Lane, District Heights, MD 20747. Visit the
company's website at http://www.h4tsmediallc.org.

ISBN: 978-0-9884278-4-6
FIRST EDITION

Cover design by David Maurice Parker,
Anointed Touch (AT) Graphics/H4TS Media, LLC
Snapshot courtesy of Chef Firecracker

9 8 7 6 5 4 3 2 1

Beverages & Appetizers

Mulled Cranberry Cider

Yield 16 servings

Ingredients:
- 2 quarts cranberry juice
- 2 oranges, zested and juiced
- 14 whole cloves
- 1 1/2 cups dried cranberries
- 1 teaspoon vanilla extract
- 1 cup honey
- 2 cinnamon sticks

Directions:
1. Pour cranberry juice into a slow cooker; set on high. To the juice add the zest and juice from the oranges, cloves, cranberries, vanilla extract, honey and cinnamon sticks. Heat, stirring occasionally, until hot and steamy, about 20 minutes.

Hot Apple Cider

Yield 6 servings

Ingredients:
- 6 cups apple cider
- 1/4 cup real maple syrup
- 2 cinnamon sticks
- 6 whole cloves
- 6 whole allspice berries
- 1 orange peel, cut into strips
- 1 lemon peel, cut into strips

Directions:
1. Pour the apple cider and maple syrup into a large stainless steel saucepan.
2. Place the cinnamon sticks, cloves, allspice berries, orange peel and lemon peel in the center of a washed square of cheesecloth; fold up the sides of the cheesecloth to enclose the bundle, and then tie it up with a length of kitchen string. Drop the spice bundle into the cider mixture.
3. Place the saucepan over moderate heat for 5 to 10 minutes, or until the cider is very hot but not boiling.
4. Remove the cider from the heat. Discard the spice bundle. Ladle the cider into big cups or mugs, adding a fresh cinnamon stick to each serving if desired.

Hot Cocoa

Yields a 1-Gallon Mix

Ingredients:
- 10 cups dry milk powder
- 4 3/4 cups sifted confectioners' sugar
- 2 1/2 cups unsweetened cocoa powder (Special Dark from Hershey's)
- 2 cups powdered non-dairy creamer
- 2 Cups of your favorite flavor powdered non-dairy creamer (optional)

Directions:
1. In a large mixing bowl, combine milk powder, confectioner's sugar, cocoa powder, and creamer. Stir till thoroughly combined. I store the cocoa mixture in an airtight gallon plastic container. It Makes about 15 cups mix, or enough for about 45 servings.
2. For 1 serving, place 1/3 cup cocoa mixture in a coffee cup or mug, and add 3/4 cup boiling water or warm milk. Stir to dissolve. Top with dollop of whipped cream or a few marshmallows, if desired.

For a different flavor variation you can add different flavor powdered creamers

Berry Smoothie

Yield 4 cups

Ingredients:
- 2 cups frozen mixed berries
- 1 cup strawberry flavored yogurt
- 1 banana, sliced
- 1 cup milk
- 1/2 teaspoon white sugar (optional)

Directions:
1. In the container of a blender combine the mixed berries, strawberry yogurt, banana, milk and sugar. Cover, and blend until smooth. Pour into glasses and serve.

Watermelon Coconut Smoothie

Yield 4 servings

Ingredients:
- 2 cups cubed frozen water melon
- 1 8 ounce can of coconut milk
- 1 8 ounce can of sweeten condensed milk
- 1 cup of ice

Directions:
1. Place all in blender and blend till smooth then enjoy. If you want the Adult touch put 3 ounces of Coconut Rum for a great cocktail.

Mango Martini

Yields 1 serving

Ingredients:
- 1/2 oz. pomegranate grape juice
- 1/2 oz. Goya mango nectar
- 1 oz. Parrot Bay Mango Rum
- 1 oz. of Smirnoff mango Vodka

Directions:
1. Place all in a shaker class with ice and shake till mixed. Strain in a chilled Martini glass and garnish with a cherry and enjoy.

Beer Cheese Fondue

Yield 6 servings

Ingredients:
- 8 ounces shredded sharp Cheddar cheese
- 8 ounces shredded gruyere cheese
- 2 tablespoons all-purpose flour
- 1/2 teaspoon salt
- 1/4 teaspoon ground black pepper
- 1 clove garlic, halved
- 1 (12 fluid ounce) can or bottle beer
- 1 dash hot pepper sauce

Directions:
1. Combine Cheddar cheese, gruyere cheese, flour, salt, and black pepper in a bowl.
2. Rub cut side of garlic clove around bottom and sides of fondue pot.
3. Pour beer into fondue pot and slowly bring to a simmer over medium-low heat, about 5 minutes.
4. Gradually stir cheese mixture into beer, adding small amounts at a time, until cheese is melted and blended, 10 to 15 minutes.
5. Stir hot pepper sauce into cheese mixture.

Black Bean Hummus

Yield 8 servings

Ingredients:
- 1 clove garlic
- 1 (15 ounce) can black beans; drain and reserve liquid
- 2 tablespoons lemon juice
- 1 1/2 tablespoons tahini
- 3/4 teaspoon ground cumin
- 1/2 teaspoon salt
- 1/4 teaspoon cayenne pepper
- 1/4 teaspoon paprika
- 10 Greek olives

Directions:
1. Mince garlic in the bowl of a food processor.
2. Add black beans, 2 tablespoons reserved liquid, 2 tablespoons lemon juice, tahini, 1/2 teaspoon cumin, 1/2 teaspoon salt, and 1/8 teaspoon cayenne pepper; process until smooth, scraping down the sides as needed.
3. Add additional seasoning and liquid to taste.
4. Garnish with paprika and Greek olives.

Serve with Pita bread or chips for a great dipping idea

Bruschetta with Shallots

Yield 8 cups

Ingredients:

- 12 roma (plum) tomatoes, chopped
- 1 tablespoon minced garlic
- 2 tablespoons minced shallots
- 1 cup chopped fresh basil leaves
- 1 teaspoon fresh lemon juice
- salt to taste
- freshly ground black pepper to taste
- 1/3 cup extra virgin olive oil
- 3 cloves garlic, cut into slivers
- 1/4 cup extra virgin olive oil
- 1 (1 pound) loaf Italian bread, cut into 1/2 inch slices

Directions:

1. In a large bowl, toss together the roma tomatoes, minced garlic, shallots, basil, lemon juice, salt, pepper and 1/3 cup olive oil.
2. Place the slivered garlic and 1/4 cup olive oil in small saucepan over medium heat. Slowly cook and stir 2 to 3 minutes. Discard garlic.
3. Toast the bread slices, and brush with the olive oil heated with garlic. Top slices with the roma tomato mixture.

Sausage Stuffed Mushrooms

Yield 4 servings

Ingredients:

- 1 1/2 lbs. medium, white button mushrooms
- 1/2 lb. Italian sausage
- 1 teaspoon fresh parsley
- 1/2 cup of shredded mozzarella cheese
- 1/4 cup of Italian style breadcrumbs

Directions:

1. Preheat oven to 450 degrees.
2. Wipe mushrooms of with a damp cloth and remove stems and chop.
3. In a skillet over medium heat, cook sausage until well browned. Remove with slotted spoon and drain meat on paper towel
4. Remove all but about 2 tablespoons of drippings from skillet. In hot drippings over medium heat cook mushroom stems until tender (about 10 minutes); stirring frequently.
5. Remove skillet from heat and stir in sausage cheese and breadcrumbs.

6. Fill mushroom caps with mixture. Place in a 15 ½ x 10 ½ -inch baking pan and bake for 15 minutes or until the top is golden brown and cheese is melted.
7. Place on serving platter and garnish with parsley.

Savory Deviled Eggs

Yield 12 deviled egg halves

Ingredients:
- 6 hard-cooked eggs, halved
- 1/4 cup mayonnaise
- 1 teaspoon rice wine vinegar
- 1/2 teaspoon chopped fresh dill
- 1 teaspoon Dijon mustard
- 1/4 teaspoon garlic powder
- 1/8 teaspoon salt
- 12 sprigs fresh dill (optional)

Directions:
1. Scoop egg yolks into a bowl and set egg whites aside.
2. Mash yolks, mayonnaise, vinegar, 1/2 teaspoon chopped dill, Dijon mustard, garlic powder, and salt. Spoon yolk mixture into egg whites.
3. Garnish with dill sprigs.
4. Refrigerate until ready to serve.

Watermelon Fire and Ice Salsa

Yield 4 cups

Ingredients:
- 3 cups chopped watermelon
- 1/2 cup chopped green bell pepper
- 2 tablespoons lime juice
- 2 tablespoons chopped fresh cilantro
- 1 tablespoon chopped green onions
- 1 tablespoon chopped jalapeno pepper
- 3 chopped garlic cloves
- salt and pepper to taste

Directions:
1. In a large bowl, combine the watermelon, green bell pepper, lime juice, cilantro, green onions, jalapeno and garlic. Add salt and pepper to taste. Mix well and serve.

Mango & Strawberry Salsa

Yield 4 cups

Ingredients:
- 1 1/2 cups chopped mangos
- 1 1/2 cups chopped Strawberries
- 1/2 cup chopped green bell pepper
- 2 tablespoons lime juice
- 2 tablespoons chopped fresh cilantro
- 1 tablespoon chopped green onions
- 1 tablespoon chopped jalapeno pepper
- 3 chopped garlic cloves
- salt and pepper to taste

Directions:
1. In a large bowl, combine the mango, strawberry, green bell pepper, lime juice, cilantro, green onions, jalapeno and garlic. Add salt and pepper to taste. Mix well and serve.

Soups, Salads & Sandwiches

<u>Insalata Caprese Salad</u>
Mozzarella, Tomato and Basil Plate - Caprese Salad Recipe

Yields: 4 servings

Ingredients:

- 1/2 pound fresh mozzarella cheese sliced 1/4-inch thick
- 2 large vine-ripened tomatoes, sliced 1/4-inch thick
- 1 cup fresh basil leaves
- Coarse salt to taste
- Freshly-ground black pepper to taste
- 2 tablespoons drained capers (optional)
- 1/4 cup extra-virgin olive oil

Directions:

1. In a circular design around the side of a serving plate, alternate fresh mozzarella slices on a large platter (or on individual plates if you are doing individual portions) with sliced tomatoes, overlapping for effect.
2. Tear fresh basil leaves and sprinkle liberally over the slices. Add salt and freshly ground pepper to taste. Sprinkle capers over the top.
3. Just before serving, drizzle on some top-quality extra-virgin olive oil. NOTE: Insalata Caprese should never be allowed to sit in oil for any length of time and become soggy, and no vinegar of any kind goes on true Insalata Caprese!

Escarole and Bean Soup

Yield 6 servings

Ingredients:

- 3 tablespoons olive oil
- 1 onion, diced
- 6 cups vegetable stock
- 3 (15 ounce) cans cannellini beans, drained and rinsed
- 1 (16 ounce) can diced tomatoes
- Salt and pepper to taste
- 2 t of crushed red pepper
- 1 pound torn escarole
- 6 cloves garlic, minced

Directions:

1. Heat the olive oil in a large pot over medium heat. Sprinkle in 1t of crushed red pepper. Stir in the onion and cook until the onion has softened and turned translucent, about 5 minutes. Add garlic and cook for 1 more minute.
2. Sauté the torn escarole, until the escarole is tender, about 10 minutes. Add salt and pepper to taste.
3. Add 3 cans of cannellini beans and cook another 5 minutes. Sprinkle in the remaining 1t of crushed red paper.
4. Add 6 cups of vegetable stock and simmer for 30 minutes or until the escarole is tender.
5. Serve with crusty bread and enjoy.

Lentil Soup

Yield 8 servings

Ingredients:

- 2 tablespoons olive oil
- 2 large onions, cubed
- 1 teaspoon minced garlic
- 3 carrots, diced
- 2 stalks celery, diced
- 3 1/2 cups crushed tomatoes
- 1 1/2 cups lentils - soaked, rinsed and drained
- 1/2 teaspoon salt
- 1/2 teaspoon ground black pepper
- 3/4 cup white wine
- 2 bay leaves
- 7 cups chicken stock or vegetable stock
- 1 sprig fresh parsley, chopped
- 1/2 teaspoon paprika
- 1/2 cup grated Parmesan cheese

Directions:

1. In a large stockpot, sauté the onions in oil until they are glossy. Stir in garlic, paprika, celery, carrots, and sauté for 10 minutes.
2. Once the vegetables have sautéed for 10 minutes stir in tomatoes, chicken stock, lentils, bay leaves, salt, and pepper. Stir well, then add the wine and bring the mixture to a boil. Slowly reduce the heat and cook for 1 hour on low to medium heat; or until the lentils are tender.
3. Sprinkle the soup with parsley and Parmesan (optional) before serving.

Pasta e Fagioli

Yield 4 servings

Ingredients:

- 1 tablespoon olive oil
- 2 stalks celery, finely chopped
- 2 medium carrots, finely chopped
- 1 medium onion, chopped
- 2 cloves garlic, minced
- 2 cups Chicken Broth or Vegetable Stock
- 1 teaspoon Italian seasoning, crushed
- 1 (14.5 ounce) can diced tomatoes, undrained
- 3/4 cup short tube-shaped ditalini pasta, cooked and drained
- 1 (15 ounce) can white kidney beans (cannellini), undrained

Directions:

1. Heat the oil in a 4-quart stockpot over medium heat. Cook the celery, carrots, onion and garlic until they're tender.
2. Stir the broth, Italian seasoning and tomatoes and beans in the stockpot. Heat to a boil. Reduce the heat to low and cook for 15 minutes or until the vegetables are tender-crisp.
3. Add the pasta and cook for 5 minutes.
4. Garnish with Parmesan cheese and enjoy with crusty bread

<u>Sangrita Soup</u>

Yield 10 servings

Ingredients:

- 2 medium ears of corn, shucked
- 4 pound(s) beefsteak tomatoes cored and coarsely chopped.
- 1 1/2 cup(s) fresh orange juice
- 1 tablespoon(s) fresh lime juice
- 1 1/2 teaspoon(s) pure ancho chile powder
- 1 teaspoon(s) pure New Mexico chile powder
- 1 tablespoon(s) grenadine syrup
- Salt to taste
- 10 oil-cured black olives, pitted and thinly sliced

Directions:

1. Bring a large saucepan of salted water to a boil. Add the corn and cook until crisp-tender, about 4 minutes. Drain and let cool. Cut the kernels from the cobs.
2. Meanwhile, in a food processor, puree the tomatoes until smooth. Pass the tomatoes through a food mill or a fine sieve set over a large bowl; you should have about 7 cups of juice.
3. Stir in the orange juice, lime juice, chile powders and the grenadine and season with salt.
4. Refrigerate until chilled, about 10 minutes.
5. Ladle the chilled soup into cups. Garnish with the olive slices and corn kernels and serve.

Split Pea and Ham Soup

Yield 8 servings

Ingredients:

- 1 pound leftover ham bone with meat attached
- 1 cup chopped onions
- 3 cloves garlic, minced
- 1 pound dried split peas
- 1 cup chopped carrots
- 2 ribs celery, diced
- 2 1/2 cups water
- 1 bay leaf
- 2 tablespoons butter
- salt and ground black pepper to taste
- 1/4 teaspoon dried marjoram leaves, crushed
- 1/4 teaspoon dried thyme leaves, crushed
- 1 quart chicken stock

Directions:

1. Place the butter in a large soup pot over medium-low heat. Stir in onion, celery, carrots and sliced garlic. Cook slowly until the onions are translucent but not brown, 5 to 8 minutes.
2. Mix in ham, bay leaf, marjoram, thyme and split peas. Pour in chicken stock and water. Stir to combine, and simmer slowly until the peas are tender and the soup is thick, about 1 hour and 15 minutes. Stir occasionally. Season with salt and black pepper to serve.

Tomato, Mozzarella & Basil Panini

A classic Italian caprese salad is reinvented as bright-flavored Panini…and it's not just for vegetarians either. Sweet heirloom tomatoes and creamy, melted fresh mozzarella are accented by fresh basil and a hint of lemon zest and olive oil on a French baguette. The result is a satisfying medley of flavors that's quick and easy to enjoy any day of the week.

Yield 1 serving

Ingredients:

- 1 French baguette, halved lengthwise
- 2-3 fresh basil leaves
- 1 heirloom tomato (or other tomato of your choice), sliced into 1/4" slices
- Lemon zest
- 2 slices fresh mozzarella cheese
- Extra-virgin olive oil
- Salt and pepper

Directions:

1. Preheat Panini grill to medium-high heat (375 degrees).
2. Drizzle olive oil inside both halves of the baguette. On the bottom half, layer basil leaves and tomatoes. Season tomatoes with salt, pepper and lemon zest. Add mozzarella and top half of baguette.
3. Grill sandwich for 5-6 minutes until cheese is melted. Serve immediately and enjoy!
4. You can use any good crusty bread I love to use ciabatta bread.

Turkey Avocado Panini

Yield 2 sandwiches

Ingredients:
- 1/2 ripe avocado
- 1/4 cup mayonnaise
- 2 ciabatta rolls
- 1 tablespoon olive oil, divided
- 2 slices provolone cheese
- 1 cup whole fresh spinach leaves, divided
- 1/4 pound thinly sliced mesquite smoked turkey breast
- 2 roasted red peppers, sliced into strips

Directions:
1. Mash the avocado and the mayonnaise together in a bowl until thoroughly mixed.
2. Preheat a Panini sandwich press.
3. To make the sandwiches, split the ciabatta rolls in half the flat way, and brush the bottom of each roll with olive oil. Place the bottoms of the rolls onto the Panini press, olive oil side down. Place a provolone cheese slice, half the spinach leaves, half the sliced turkey breast, and a sliced roasted red pepper on each sandwich. Spread half of the avocado mixture on the cut surface of each top, and place the top of the roll on the sandwich. Brush the top of the roll with olive oil.
4. Close the Panini press and cook until the bun is toasted and crisp, with golden brown grill marks, and the cheese has melted, about 5 to 8 minutes.

Sauces & Sides

Apple-Chestnut Puree

Yield 16 servings

Ingredients:

- 4 cups chopped peeled Granny Smith apple (about 1 1/2 pounds)
- 1 cup bottled chestnuts
- 1/2 cup Calvados (apple brandy)
- 1/3 cup packed brown sugar
- 2 tablespoons maple syrup
- 2 tablespoons half-and-half
- 2 tablespoons Calvados (apple brandy)
- 1/2 teaspoon salt
- 1 teaspoon finely chopped fresh sage

Directions:

1. To prepare puree, while roast bakes, combine apple, chestnuts, 1/2 cup Calvados, sugar, and 2 tablespoons syrup in a medium saucepan; bring to a boil.
2. Reduce heat, and simmer 15 minutes or until apple is tender.
3. Place mixture in a food processor; add half-and-half, 2 tablespoons Calvados, 1/2 teaspoon, salt, and chopped sage. Process 1 minute or until smooth.
4. Serve with pork

Bolognese Sauce - Traditional Italian Meat-Based Sauce for Pasta

Yield 8-10 servings

Ingredients:

- 2 tablespoons extra virgin olive oil
- 1 green peppers, seeded and diced
- 2 medium carrots, peeled and diced
- 3 stalks of celery diced
- 1 medium yellow onions, peeled and diced
- 4 -6 garlic cloves, peeled and diced
- 1/2 lb. of ground pork
- 1/2 lb. of ground veal
- 3/4 lb. ground beef
- 1 1/2 cups dry red wine
- 1 cup beef broth
- 1 pinch allspice
- 1 teaspoon dried thyme
- 1 teaspoon dried basil
- 1 teaspoon dried oregano
- fresh ground pepper and salt to taste
- 1 (28 ounce) cans whole tomatoes with juice, chopped fine

Directions:

1. Over a medium flame, heat the olive oil in a large, sauté pan. To the pan add the diced vegetables, sauté for 6 or 7 minutes until the onions turn clear and the garlic starts to "dance". Pour all ingredients into a large bowl; reserve for later.
2. Continuing to cook over a medium flame, add the ground pork, veal, and beef to the sauté pan, breaking into bite-sized pieces with a fork while it cooks; stir often. Sprinkle with 1/2 teaspoon salt; cook until no longer pink.
3. Lower your flame to medium-low and return the sautéed vegetables to the sauté pan; gently stir together to blend. Add the wine and simmer until the alcohol evaporates, about 3 minutes, add the allspice, basil, oregano and pepper. Simmer for 3 or 4 minutes.
4. Stir in the tomatoes and juice. When the sauce starts to boil, reduce the heat so that it cooks at the barest simmer, with just an occasional bubble or two. Cook, uncovered, for 3 hours, turning down the heat if the sauce starts to scorch. If the sauce dries out before it is done, add a ladle beef broth; and check the seasoning.
5. The sauce will improve steadily as it cooks, and if you have the time simmer it longer - many Italian cooks suggest that it be simmered for 6 hours, adding the tomato juice or broth as necessary. When this Bolognese sauce is done, it should be rich and thick.
6. Serve over your favorite pasta or spaghetti and enjoy with garlic bread.

Pomodoro Pasta Sauce

Yield 8 Cups

Ingredients:

- 1/2 (28 ounce) can diced tomatoes
- 1 stalk celery, with leaves, chopped
- 1 carrots, peeled and chopped
- 1/2 small sweet onion, chopped
- 1-1/2 cloves garlic
- 1/4 (6 ounce) can tomato paste
- 1 cup water or vegetable stock

- 1 cup red wine
- 1/2 teaspoon dried sage
- 1/2 teaspoon dried basil
- 1/2 teaspoon dried parsley
- 1-1/2 teaspoons dried oregano
- salt and ground black pepper to taste

Directions:

1. Stir the diced tomatoes, celery, carrots, sweet onion, garlic, tomato paste, water, red wine, sage, basil, parsley, oregano, salt, and pepper together in a large pot and bring to a boil. Reduce heat to low and cook the sauce at a simmer until the carrots are tender, about 1 hour.
2. Pour the sauce into a blender, filling the pitcher no more than halfway. Hold the lid of the blender in place with a towel and carefully start the blender using a few quick pulses to get the sauce moving before leaving it on to puree. Puree in batches until smooth and pour into a clean container. Alternately, you can use a stick blender and puree the sauce in the pot.

Tasty Pasta Sauce

Yield 8 servings

Ingredients:

- 1 small onion, finely chopped
- 1 tablespoon of olive oil
- 2 teaspoons salt
- 3 teaspoons pepper
- 3 cloves garlic, minced
- 1 (6 ounce) can tomato paste
- 1 (28 ounce) can tomato puree
- 2 cups of merlot
- 1 (15 ounce) can diced tomatoes
- 2 teaspoons dried thyme
- 4 teaspoons dried basil leaves
- 2 teaspoons dried rosemary
- 1-1/2 teaspoons dried marjoram
- 2 teaspoons crushed bay leaf

Directions:

1. In a large saucepan add onion, and cook until soft and translucent. Season with salt and pepper. Stir in garlic and cook for 1 minute.
2. Add tomato puree, diced tomatoes, tomato paste and merlot. Season with thyme, basil, rosemary, marjoram and bay leaf.
3. Cover, and simmer on low heat for 1 hour.

* Enjoy with pasta of your choice and garlic bread for a complete meal. You can always add cooked meatballs and sausage to the sauce for a bolder flavor and a heartier meal.*

Basic Risotto Recipe

Yields 6-8 servings

Ingredients:

- 1½ cups Arborio rice
- 1 qtr. chicken stock or vegetable broth
- ½ cup white wine
- 1 medium shallot or ½ small onion, chopped (about ½ cup)
- 3 tablespoons unsalted butter
- 1 tablespoons vegetable oil or olive oil
- ¼ cup grated Parmesan cheese
- 1 tablespoons chopped Italian parsley
- Kosher salt, to taste

Directions:

1. Heat the stock to a simmer in a medium saucepan, and then lower the heat so that the stock just stays hot.
2. In a large, heavy-bottomed saucepan, heat the oil and 1 Tbsp. of the butter over medium heat. When the butter has melted, add the chopped shallot or onion. Sauté for 2-3 minutes or until it is slightly translucent.
3. Add the rice to the pot and stir it briskly with a wooden spoon so that the grains are coated with the oil and melted butter. Sauté for another minute or so, until there is a slightly nutty aroma. But don't let the rice turn brown.
4. Add the wine and cook while stirring, until the liquid is fully absorbed.
5. Add a ladle of hot chicken stock to the rice and stir until the liquid is fully absorbed. When the rice appears almost dry, add another ladle of stock and repeat the process. ****Note:** It's important to stir constantly, especially while the hot stock gets absorbed, to prevent scorching, and add the next ladle as soon as the rice is almost dry.**
6. Continue adding ladles of hot stock and stirring the rice while the liquid is absorbed. As it cooks, you'll see that the rice will take on a creamy consistency as it begins to release its natural starches.
7. Continue adding stock, a ladle at a time, for 20-30 minutes or until the grains are tender but still firm to the bite, without being crunchy. If you run out of stock and the risotto still isn't done, you can finish the cooking using hot water. Just add the water as you did with the stock, a ladle at a time, stirring while it's absorbed.
8. Stir in the remaining 2 Tbsp. butter, the parmesan cheese and the parsley, and season to taste with kosher salt.
9. Risotto turns glutinous if held for too long; you should serve it right away. A properly cooked risotto should form a soft, creamy mound on a dinner plate. It shouldn't run across the plate, nor should it be stiff or gluey.

Cilantro-Lime Rice

Yield 6 servings

Ingredients:
- 1 cup long grain white rice
- 2 cups of chicken stock
- 2 tablespoons fresh lime juice
- 2 tablespoons chopped fresh cilantro
- salt to taste

Directions:
1. Bring the rice, chicken stock to a boil in a saucepan over high heat.
2. Reduce heat to medium-low, cover, and simmer until the rice is tender, 20 to 25 minutes.
3. Remove from the heat, add the lime juice, cilantro, and salt; fluff with a fork and serve.

Mushroom Orzo

Yield 6 servings

Ingredients:
- 1/2 cup butter, divided
- 8 pearl onions
- 1 cup uncooked orzo pasta
- 1/2 cup sliced fresh mushrooms
- 1 cup water
- 1/2 cup white wine
- garlic powder to taste
- salt and pepper to taste
- 1/2 cup grated Parmesan cheese
- 1/4 cup fresh parsley

Directions:
1. Melt 1/2 the butter in a skillet over medium heat. Stir in the onions, and cook until golden brown. Mix in orzo, mushrooms, and remaining butter. Cook and stir 5 minutes, until butter is melted and mushrooms are tender.
2. Stir in wine into the skillet and cook for 2 minutes then add water and bring to a boil. Reduce heat to low. Season with garlic powder, salt, and pepper. Cook 7 to 10 minutes, until orzo is al dente. Stir in the Parmesan cheese and parsley to serve.

Main Entrees

Fettuccini with Mushroom, Ham and Rose Sauce

Yield 8 servings

Ingredients:

- 1 pound dry fettuccine pasta
- 2 tablespoons of olive oil
- 1/2 cup finely diced onion
- 3 cloves garlic, minced
- 1 pound fresh sliced mushrooms
- 2 teaspoons dried oregano
- 2 teaspoons dried basil
- 2 teaspoons dried parsley
- Salt and pepper to taste
- 6 slices ham, chopped
- 1 1/2 cups heavy whipping cream
- 1 cup spaghetti sauce
- 1 teaspoon crushed red pepper (optional)

Directions:

1. Bring a large pot of lightly salted water to a boil. Add pasta and cook for 8 to 10 minutes or until al dente; drain.
2. In a large sauté pan, melt the butter over medium heat. Add the onion and garlic and cook until softened. Stir in the sliced mushrooms and the oregano, basil, and parsley. Cook, stirring occasionally, until the liquid from the mushrooms has evaporated. Add the ham pieces and cook for another 4 to 5 minutes.
3. Pour in the heavy cream and bring to a boil. Slowly stir in the spaghetti sauce and crushed red pepper (optional) blending it into the cream. Cook, stirring occasionally, until the sauce has reduced by a third and is thick.
4. Place fettuccini on plates and ladle even portions of sauce over top.

Gnocchi with Zucchini Ribbons
&
Parsley Brown Butter

Yields 4 servings

Ingredients:

- 1 pound fresh or frozen gnocchi
- 2 tablespoons butter
- 2 medium shallots chopped
- 1 pound zucchini (about 3 small), very thinly sliced lengthwise (see Tip)
- 1 pint cherry tomatoes , halved

- 2 cloves of minced garlic
- 1/2 teaspoon salt
- 1/4 teaspoon grated nutmeg
- Freshly ground pepper to taste
- 1/2 cup grated Parmesan cheese
- 1/2 cup chopped fresh parsley

Directions:

1. Bring a large saucepan of water to a boil. Cook gnocchi according to package instructions until they float, 3 to 5 minutes. Drain.
2. Meanwhile, melt butter in a large skillet over medium-high heat. Cook until the butter is beginning to brown, about 2 minutes.
3. Add garlic, shallots and zucchini and cook, stirring often, until softened, 2 to 3 minutes. Add cherry tomatoes, salt, nutmeg and pepper and continue cooking, stirring often, until the tomatoes are just starting to break down, 1 to 2 minutes.
4. Stir in Parmesan and parsley.
5. Add gnocchi and toss to coat. Serve immediately.

Tip: To make "ribbon-thin" zucchini, slice lengthwise with a vegetable peeler or on a mandoline slicer.

Pasta with Roasted Vegetables

Yield 6 servings

Ingredients:

- 1/2 pound pasta such as radiatore (also called 'nuggets')
- 1 yellow squash cut into half circles
- 1 zucchini cut into half circles
- 1 bunch green onions - cut into 1 1/2 inch lengths
- 1/2 pound baby carrots - cut in half lengthwise
- 1/2 pound green beans cut in half

- 3 cloves of garlic - minced
- 1/4 cup olive oil
- 1 teaspoon Kosher or sea salt
- 1 teaspoon of black pepper
- 1/2 cup vegetable or chicken stock
- 2 Tablespoons lemon juice
- 1/2 teaspoon dried basil – crushed
- 1/2 teaspoon of chopped fresh basil or parsley for garnishing

Directions:

1. Preheat oven to 450 degrees F.
2. Toss vegetables with garlic, olive oil and salt and pepper. Spread evenly onto a parchment covered baking sheet.
3. Roast for 25 to 30 minutes, checking every 10 minutes to stir and keep from burning.
4. While vegetables are roasting, cook pasta until desired doneness is reached.
5. When vegetables are done, drain pasta and combine pasta and vegetables with stock and lemon juice mixture. Toss to coat, add salt and pepper if needed and serve hot and garnish with fresh basil or parsley.

Red Pepper-Salmon Pasta

Yield 4 servings

Ingredients:
- 4 (4 ounce) fillets salmon
- 2 tablespoons lemon juice
- 1/2 cup roasted red bell peppers
- 1/3 cup grated Parmesan cheese
- 1 tablespoon cornstarch
- 2 teaspoons minced jalapeno peppers
- 1 clove garlic, minced
- 1/4 cup chopped fresh cilantro
- 1 cup chicken broth
- 1 (8 ounce) package angel hair pasta

Directions:
1. In an 8 inch baking dish, arrange filets in a single layer. Sprinkle with lemon juice. Tightly cover dish with foil. Bake at 450 degrees F (230 degrees C). Cook until fish is opaque, but still moist looking in thickest part, 12 to 14 minutes.
2. Meanwhile, in a blender, smoothly puree red peppers, parmesan, cornstarch, chili, and garlic. Add cilantro and chicken broth; whirl to blend.
3. Pour pepper mixture into a 10 inch frying pan. Stir over high heat until boiling. Reduce heat to keep warm.
4. Cook pasta in 3 quarts boiling water until tender to bite, about 7 minutes. Drain, and return to pan.
5. Stir juices from the baked salmon into red pepper sauce. Mix 1 1/2 cups sauce with pasta. Spoon pasta onto plates and top with fish, and drizzle with remaining sauce.

Chicken Parmesan

Yield 4 servings

Ingredients:

- 1 1/2 cup Italian-seasoned breadcrumbs
- 3 tablespoons all-purpose flour
- 1/2 teaspoon ground red pepper
- 4 skinned and boned chicken breasts
- 3 egg, lightly beaten
- 1 tablespoon olive oil
- Tomato Sauce
- 1 1/2 cup shredded mozzarella cheese
- 1/2 cup freshly grated Parmesan cheese

Directions:

1. Combine breadcrumbs, flour, and ground red pepper in a small bowl, and set aside.
2. Place chicken between two sheets of heavy-duty plastic wrap, and flatten to 1/4-inch thickness, using a meat mallet or rolling pin.
3. Dip 1 chicken breast in egg whites, and coat with breadcrumb mixture. Dip again in egg mixture, and coat again in breadcrumb mixture.
4. Repeat procedure with remaining chicken breast.
5. Cook chicken in hot oil over medium heat 2 to 3 minutes on each side or until done.
6. Place chicken breasts in a single layer in a lightly greased 8-inch square baking dish. Top evenly with Tomato Sauce and cheeses.
7. Bake at 350° for 20 minutes or until cheeses melt.

Lemon-Rosemary Chicken

Yield 4 Servings

Ingredients:
- 2 lemon, zest and juiced
- 1 4-lb. whole chicken or cut up chicken pieces, rinsed and patted dry
- 3 sprigs fresh rosemary
- 2 cloves garlic
- 3 tablespoons of Olive oil
- Salt and pepper

Directions:
1. Place chicken on a roasting pan breast side up. Fold wings under and tie legs together if using whole chicken if using parts just place in a baking dish.
2. For marinade place mince garlic, rosemary, lemon zest and juice, add a pinch of salt and pepper in a small bowl and whisk in olive oil and rub on whole chicken or pieces and let marinade for 2 hours or overnight.
3. Preheat oven to 375 degrees and cook for a total of 1 hour for whole chicken or 45 minutes for chicken pieces or until juices run clear and a meat thermometer reads 165 degrees for a total of 15 seconds.
4. Let the whole chicken rest for 10 minutes on a cutting board before carving and serving.
5. For a grilling option make extra marinade. Heat grill to 400 degrees and place cut up pieces on grill and cook for 45 minutes turning occasional and basting with extra marinade.

** Remember to make sure chicken is cooked to an internal temperature of 165 degrees**

Maple-Mustard Glazed Chicken

Yield 4 Servings

Ingredients:

- 2 teaspoons olive oil
- 4 (6-ounce) skinless, boneless chicken breast halves
- 1/2 teaspoon freshly ground black pepper
- 1/4 teaspoon salt
- 1 tablespoon stone-ground mustard
- 1/4 cup fat-free, lower-sodium chicken broth
- 1/4 cup maple syrup
- 2 teaspoons chopped fresh thyme
- 2 medium garlic cloves, thinly sliced
- 1 tablespoon cider vinegar

Directions:

1. Preheat oven to 400°.
2. Heat a large ovenproof skillet over medium-high heat. Add oil; swirl to coat. Sprinkle chicken with pepper and salt. Add chicken to pan; sauté 2 minutes on each side or until browned.
3. Remove chicken from pan. Add broth, syrup, thyme, and garlic to pan; bring to a boil, scraping pan to loosen browned bits. Cook 2 minutes, stirring frequently. Add vinegar and mustard; cook for 1 minute, stirring constantly.
4. Return chicken to pan and spoon mustard mixture over chicken.
5. Bake at 400° for 10 minutes or until the chicken is done.
6. Remove chicken from pan; let stand 5 minutes. Place pan over medium heat; cook mustard mixture 2 minutes or until liquid is syrupy, stirring frequently. Serve with chicken.

Italian Meatballs

Yield 30 meatballs

Ingredients:

- 1/3 cup Italian style bread crumbs
- 2 tablespoons olive oil
- 1 onion, grated
- 2 pound ground beef
- 2 eggs
- 1/4 bunch fresh parsley, chopped
- 3 cloves garlic, crushed

- 2 teaspoons salt
- 1 teaspoon ground black pepper
- 1 tablespoon dried Italian herb seasoning
- 2 tablespoons grated Parmesan cheese

Directions:

1. Cover a baking sheet with foil and spray lightly with cooking spray.
2. Soak bread crumbs in milk in a small bowl for 20 minutes.
3. Heat olive oil in a skillet over medium heat. Cook and stir onions in hot oil until translucent, about 20 minutes.
4. In a large bowl stir onions, bread crumbs, eggs, parsley, garlic, salt, black pepper, Italian herb seasoning, and Parmesan cheese into ground beef with a rubber spatula until combined. Cover and refrigerate for about one hour.
5. Preheat an oven to 425 degrees F (220 degrees C).
6. Using wet hands, form meat mixture into balls about 1 1/2 inches in diameter. Arrange onto prepared baking sheet. (I prefer to use a cookie scoop to keep my hands clean.)
7. Bake in the preheated oven until browned and cooked through, 15 to 20 minutes turning occasionally.

Picadillo
Classic Cuban-Style ground beef dish

Yield 4 servings

Ingredients:

- 2 teaspoons olive oil
- 3 cloves garlic, chopped
- 1 small chopped onion
- 1 medium green bell pepper chopped
- 1 pound lean ground beef
- 1 (5 ounce) jar green olives, pitted and halved
- 1 (3.5 ounce) jar of capers with liquid
- 1/2 cup of raisins
- 2 tablespoon white vinegar
- 1/4 teaspoon of salt
- 1 teaspoon freshly ground black pepper
- 1 teaspoon white sugar
- 1 tablespoon of cumin
- 1 tablespoon of coriander
- 1 (8 ounce) can of tomato sauce

Directions:

1. Heat olive oil in a skillet over medium heat; cook and stir garlic, onion, and green bell pepper in the hot oil until softened, 5 to 7 minutes.
2. Crumble ground beef into the skillet; cook and stir until browned completely, 7 to 10 minutes.
3. Stir olives, raisins, capers, vinegar, tomato sauce, cumin, coriander, sugar, salt, and pepper through the ground beef mixture.
4. Cover the skillet; reduce heat to low, and cook until the mixture is heated through, 5 to 10 minutes.

Enjoy with white or yellow rice and black beans for a complete meal
** You can also substitute Morning Star Farms Meatless Crumbles instead of ground beef for a vegetarian option**

Rosemary Flank Steak

Yield 6 servings

Ingredients:

- 1 tablespoon chopped fresh rosemary
- 2 garlic cloves, minced
- 3/4 teaspoon kosher salt
- 1/2 teaspoon freshly ground pepper
- 3 tablespoons olive oil
- 1 (1 1/4-lb.) flank steak

Directions:

1. Stir together first 4 ingredients and 1 Tbsp. olive oil. Rub onto steak; cover and chill 30 minutes to 4 hours.
2. Preheat grill to 400° to 450° (high) heat.
3. Grill steak, covered with grill lid, 5 minutes on each side or to desired degree of doneness. Let stand 5 minutes.
4. Cut steak diagonally across the grain into thin strips, and arrange on a serving platter.

Sunday Beef and Gravy

Yield 6 serving

Ingredients:

- 3 tablespoons vegetable oil
- 1 onion, diced
- 2 pounds cubed beef stew meat
- 3 cups of beef broth
- 2 teaspoons of flour
- 2 teaspoons of Italian seasoning
- 3 cloves of fresh garlic grated
- 1 tablespoon salt
- 2 teaspoon ground black pepper

Directions:

1. Place beef in a slow cooker and add onion, garlic, Italian seasoning, salt and pepper and flour and mix all together to coat the meat. Cover beef with broth.
2. Cover, set slow cooker to High, and cook for 1 hour; turn cooker down to Low and cook for 5 more hours. During cooking check for additional seasoning if necessary and season to taste.

**Enjoy over egg noodles, rice or even mashed potatoes for a hearty meal. **

Veal Marsala

Yield 4 servings

Ingredients:

- 4 (6-ounce) Veal cutlets
- 1/4 teaspoon salt
- 1/4 teaspoon freshly ground black pepper
- 2 tablespoons all-purpose flour
- 1 tablespoon olive oil
- 1 tablespoon of butter
- 1 cup pre sliced mushroom
- 2 tablespoons fresh lemon juice
- 1/2 cup Marsala wine
- 1/2 cup fat-free, less-sodium chicken broth
- 1 tablespoon chopped fresh parsley

Directions:

1. Sprinkle both sides of Veal evenly with salt and pepper. Place flour in a shallow dish. Dredge veal in flour, turning to coat; shake off excess flour.
2. Heat olive oil and butter in a large skillet over medium-high heat. Add veal; cook 2 minutes on each side or until browned.
3. Remove veal from pan; keep warm. Add mushrooms, wine, broth, and juice to pan; reduce heat, and simmer 10 minutes or until mixture is reduced to 2/3 cup.
4. Return veal to pan, turning to coat well. Cover and cook 5 minutes or until veal is done. Sprinkle with parsley.

Apricot Ginger Pork Chops

Yield 4 servings

Ingredients:

- Cooking spray
- 4 (4-ounce) boneless loin pork chops
- 1 teaspoon minced ginger
- 1/4 cup onion chopped
- 1/4 cup apricot preserves
- 2 tablespoon low-sodium soy sauce
- 2 teaspoons minced garlic
- salt and pepper
- 1/4 cup sliced green onions

Directions:

1. Heat a large nonstick skillet over medium-high heat. Coat pan with cooking spray.
2. Sprinkle salt and pepper on both sides.
3. Add pork to pan; cook 6 minutes on each side or until done. Remove from pan; keep warm.
4. Add chopped onion to pan; sauté 4 minutes or until lightly browned. Stir in preserves, soy sauce, garlic, ginger and salt and pepper to taste; cook 3 minutes or until thickened.
5. Add pork to pan, turning to coat. Sprinkle with green onions.

Fennel-Crusted Pork Tenderloin

Yield 4 servings

Ingredients:

- 2 tablespoons fennel seeds
- 1 tablespoon coriander seeds
- 6 tablespoons fat-free, less-sodium chicken broth, divided
- 1 tablespoon Worcestershire sauce
- 1 teaspoon minced garlic
- 1/4 teaspoon salt
- 1/8 teaspoon freshly ground black pepper
- 1 (1-pound) pork tenderloin, trimmed
- 2 teaspoons olive oil

Directions:

1. Place fennel and coriander in a spice or coffee grinder; process until coarsely ground. Place spice mixture in a blender or food processor. Add 2 tablespoons broth, Worcestershire sauce, garlic, salt, and pepper; process until well-blended.
2. Slice the pork tenderloin horizontally into 2 equal pieces. Slice each piece of pork lengthwise, cutting to, but not through, other side; open flat. Rub spice mixture over pork.
3. Heat olive oil in a large nonstick skillet over medium heat. Add pork; cook 5 minutes on each side or until done. Remove pork from pan; keep warm. Add 1/4 cup broth to pan, and cook until liquid almost evaporates, scraping the pan to loosen browned bits. Pour over pork.

Maple and Calvados-Glazed Crown Pork Roast with Apple-Chestnut Puree

Yield 16 servings

Ingredients:
- 1/2 cup Calvados (apple brandy)
- 1/4 cup maple syrup
- 1 sage sprig
- 1 (16-rib) crown roast of pork (about 10 1/4 pounds), trimmed
- 2 tablespoons of olive oil
- 1 1/2 teaspoons salt
- 1 teaspoon freshly ground black pepper
- Cooking spray

Directions:
1. Preheat oven to 450°.
2. To prepare roast, combine 1/2 cup Calvados, 1/4 cup syrup, and sage sprig in a small saucepan; bring to a boil over medium-high heat. Reduce heat; simmer 5 minutes or until slightly thick. Remove from heat; discard sage sprig.
3. Rub with olive oil; 1 1/2 teaspoons salt and pepper over roast. Place roast on a broiler pan coated with cooking spray. Brush one-fourth of glaze over roast. Bake at 450° for 25 minutes or until browned.
4. Reduce oven temperature to 300° (do not remove roast from oven); bake at 300° for 1 hour and 45 minutes, brushing with glaze every 30 minutes. (Cover bones with foil if they start to become too brown).
5. Increase oven temperature to 400° (do not remove roast from oven); cook an additional 25 minutes or until a thermometer inserted in meaty part of roast registers 150°. Remove roast from oven; let stand 20 minutes before carving.
6. Slice vertically between each rib bone. Serve pork with puree.

See recipe for Apple Chestnut Puree

Roasted Pork Chops with Sweet Potatoes & Apples

Yield 4 servings

Ingredients:

- 4-3 oz. boneless pork chops
- 4small sweet potatoes
- 2 medium size apple
- 1 small onion
- 2 tablespoons cinnamon

- 2 Tablespoons ground nutmeg
- 2 tablespoons ground ginger
- 3 teaspoons sugar
- 2 teaspoons cayenne or red pepper
- Salt

Directions:

1. Season pork chops with red pepper, salt and brown on both sides.
2. Slice Sweet potatoes, apple, and onion and season with sugar, cinnamon, ginger and nutmeg.
3. Bake pork chops and sweet potato / apple mixture uncovered in a cast iron skillet or casserole dish at 420 degrees for about 25 minutes.

Aromatic Swordfish Steaks

Yield 4 servings

Ingredients:

- 3/4 cup plain yogurt
- 1 tablespoon Jamaican jerk seasoning (See Recipe)
- 1 tablespoon fresh lemon juice
- 1 teaspoon garlic powder
- 1 teaspoon ground cumin

- 1 teaspoon chili powder
- 1/2 teaspoon ground cinnamon
- 1/2 teaspoon ground ginger
- 4 (6-ounce) swordfish steaks (about 3/4 inch thick)
- Cooking spray

Directions:

1. Combine the first 8 ingredients in a large bowl. Add fish, turning to coat. Cover and refrigerate for 1 hour, turning the bag occasionally.
2. Prepare grill.
3. Place fish on grill rack coated with cooking spray; grill 4 minutes on each side or until fish flakes easily when tested with a fork or until desired degree of doneness

Grilled King Salmon with Tomato-Peach Salsa

Yield 4 servings

Ingredients:

- 1 cup chopped peeled peach
- 3/4 cup quartered cherry tomatoes
- 1/4 cup thinly vertically sliced red onion
- 3 tablespoons small fresh mint leaves
- 3 tablespoons small fresh basil leaves
- 2 tablespoons fresh lemon juice
- 1 tablespoon extra-virgin olive oil
- 1 tablespoon honey
- 1 jalapeño pepper, thinly sliced (optional)
- 1 teaspoon kosher salt, divided
- 4 (6-ounce) wild Alaskan king salmon fillets
- 1/4 teaspoon freshly ground black pepper
- Cooking spray

Directions:

1. Preheat grill to high heat.
2. Combine first 8 ingredients in a bowl; add jalapeño, if desired. Sprinkle mixture with 1/4 teaspoon salt; toss gently.
3. Sprinkle fillets evenly with remaining 3/4 teaspoon salt and black pepper.
4. Place the fillets on a grill rack coated with cooking spray, and grill for 10 minutes or until desired degree of doneness, turning after 5 minutes. Serve with salsa.

Grilled Lime Shrimp

Yields 6 servings

Ingredients:
- 3 pound jumbo shrimp, uncooked
- 4 large garlic cloves, minced
- 1 teaspoon coarse or sea salt
- 1/2 teaspoon black pepper
- 6 tablespoons fresh-squeezed lime juice
- 3/4 cup extra-virgin olive oil

Directions:
1. Preheat barbecue grill (oil hot grill to help prevent sticking).
2. In the food processor, place minced garlic, salt, pepper, lime juice, and olive oil; blend until smooth and emulsified.
3. Peel and devein the shrimp, leaving the tails on. Place deveined shrimp in a large bowl. Toss shrimp with the lime marinade. NOTE: Do not leave the shrimp in the marinade for more than 15 minutes, as the texture of the shrimp will change. The lime juice will actually start cooking the shrimp.
4. After marinating the shrimp and ready to cook, place the marinated shrimp onto the hot grill and cook approximately 3 minutes (depending on size of the shrimp) on one side; turn and cook another 2 to 3 minutes or until shrimp are opaque in center (cut to test). Remove from grill.

*To serve, arrange shrimp on a large serving platter with cilantro lime rice and enjoy! *

Lemon Garlic Tilapia

Yield 4 servings

Ingredients:
- 4 Tilapia fillets
- 1 tbsp. olive oil
- 1 tbsp. Country Crock Shed's Spread
- Juice of 1 lemon
- 1 tsp. dried parsley flakes
- Dash of salt
- Cayenne pepper to taste
- 1 tsp. garlic powder

Directions:
1. Preheat oven to 400.
2. Spray a baking dish with non-stick cooking spray.
3. Melt butter in microwave.
4. Add olive oil, lemon juice, garlic powder, salt and parsley and sauté for a few minutes.
5. Pour over tilapia fillets in baking pan.
6. Sprinkle some cayenne pepper on top of fish.
7. Bake in preheated oven for about 13 minutes, and broil for an additional 2-3 minutes.

Breakfast & Breads

Zucchini and Potato Frittata

Yield 4-8 servings

Ingredients:

- 6 large eggs
- splash of milk, cream or water
- 1 small zucchini, sliced into half moons
- 1 medium potato, sliced same as zucchini
- 1 tsp. garlic powder
- 1 small onion, sliced
- 1 tsp. Italian seasoning
- Shredded cheese (mozzarella, cheddar etc.)
- Parmesan cheese
- salt and pepper
- 2 tbsp. Olive Oil

Directions:

1. Preheat oven to 375 degrees.
2. Beat eggs with milk, parmesan cheese and season with salt and pepper. Then set it aside.
3. In an oven safe 4-10 inch sauté pan sauté potato, zucchini and onions in plenty of oil until cooked through and season with salt, pepper, Italian seasoning and garlic powder (it doesn't need to brown).
4. Add egg mixture to pan. As eggs begin to cook pull cooked egg away from the side of the pan and let raw egg move into its place, as if making scrambled eggs. Once eggs start to cook a little and cheese.
5. Once the first side is cooked and there are no runny ends and the middle is set sprinkle cheese on top and finish cooking in the oven for 10-15 minutes or until the second side is cooked. I like to broil the top till lightly browned. Transfer to a plate. Cut like a pie and serve with crusty bread.

<u>Basic Scones</u>

Yield 1 Dozen

Ingredients:
- 2 cups flour
- 4 teaspoons baking powder
- 3/4 teaspoon salt
- 1/3 cup sugar
- 6 tablespoons butter (keep very cold for best use)
- 3/4 cup cream
- 1 egg

Directions:
1. Heat oven to 375 degrees.
2. In a large mixing bowl, combine flour, baking powder, salt and sugar. Mix well. Cut in butter and shortening.
3. In a separate bowl, combine cream with beaten egg then add to dry ingredients. Turn dough out onto a floured surface.
4. Roll dough out and cut into biscuit size rounds. Bake for 15 minutes or until brown.

You can add any flavor either savory or sweet. I love scones with dried fruit or chocolate chips

Blueberry Muffins

Yield 8 Large Muffins

Ingredients:

- 1 1/2 cups all-purpose flour
- 3/4 cup white sugar
- 1/2 teaspoon salt
- 2 teaspoons baking powder
- 1/3 cup vegetable oil
- 1 egg

- 1/3 cup milk
- 1 cup fresh blueberries
- 1/2 cup white sugar
- 1/3 cup all-purpose flour
- 1/4 cup butter, cubed
- 1 1/2 teaspoons ground cinnamon

Directions:

1. Preheat oven to 400 degrees F (200 degrees C). Grease muffin cups or line with muffin liners.
2. Combine 1 1/2 cups flour, 3/4 cup sugar, salt and baking powder. Place vegetable oil into a 1 cup measuring cup; add the egg and enough milk to fill the cup. Mix this with flour mixture. Fold in blueberries. Fill muffin cups right to the top, and sprinkle with crumb topping mixture.
3. To Make Crumb Topping: Mix together 1/2 cup sugar, 1/3 cup flour, 1/4 cup butter, and 1 1/2 teaspoons cinnamon. Mix with fork, and sprinkle over muffins before baking.
4. Bake for 20 to 25 minutes in the preheated oven, or until done.

Spiced Pumpkin Pancakes

Yield 6 servings

Ingredients:

- 2 cups pastry flour
- 4 teaspoons baking powder
- 1 teaspoons baking soda
- .5 teaspoons ground nutmeg
- .5 teaspoons ground ginger
- .25 cup brown sugar

- 1 egg yolk
- 2 cups 2% milk
- 1 cup canned pumpkin
- 3 tablespoons apple butter
- 3 egg whites

Directions:

1. In a large bowl, whisk together the flour, baking powder, baking soda, and spices.
2. In a separate bowl, mix together the egg yolk, pumpkin, brown sugar, and apple butter. Stir in milk until well-blended.
3. All at once, add milk mixture to dry ingredients and stir just until combined.
4. In a medium bowl, beat egg whites until light and fluffy (you can use a fork, whisk, or electric beater for this). Fold egg whites into batter.
5. Ladle batter by ¼-cup amounts onto a preheated nonstick griddle lightly sprayed with cooking spray, Cook until evenly browned on both sides.

**Recipe makes 20 pancakes (when the 1/4 cup measure is used). **

Basic Waffles

Yield 4 to 5 waffles

Ingredients:
- 1¾ cups all-purpose flour
- 2 tsp. baking powder
- ½ tsp. salt
- 1 Tbsp. granulated sugar

- 3 eggs
- 1¾ cups whole milk
- ½ cup vegetable oil
- ½ tsp. pure vanilla extract (optional)

Directions:
1. Pre-heat your waffle iron to its hottest setting. Placing a cookie-sheet under it can help catch any dripping batter during cooking.
2. Pre-heat oven to 200°F.
3. Sift together flour, baking powder and salt.
4. Beat eggs thoroughly. Whisk in sugar, milk and oil.
5. Add liquid ingredients to dry ingredients and mix gently until combined. Don't over mix!
6. Spray both surfaces of your waffle iron with cooking spray.
7. Ladle 4 to 6 oz. (½ to ¾ cup) batter on the iron and close it. It's not unusual for a bit of batter to seep out of the edges of the iron. If there's excessive leakage, use less batter for the next waffle.
8. Cook until the waffle irons indicator light shows that cooking is complete, or until no more steam comes out. The finished waffle should be golden brown and crispy.
9. Lift the waffle out of the iron with a pair of tongs and either serve right away or transfer it to the oven to keep warm.

I love to add blueberries or chocolate chips to the batter for different variations
I also top the waffles with ice cream and chocolate sauce for a dessert variation

Ciabatta Bread

Yield 2 loaves

Ingredients:

- 1/8 teaspoon active dry yeast
- 2 tablespoons warm water (110 degrees F/45 degrees C)
- 1/3 cup warm water
- 1 cup bread flour
- 1/2 teaspoon active dry yeast

- 2 tablespoons warm milk (110 degrees F/45 degrees C)
- 2/3 cup warm water
- 1 tablespoon olive oil
- 2 cups bread flour
- 1 1/2 teaspoons salt

Directions:

1. To Make Sponge: In a small bowl stir together 1/8 teaspoon of the yeast and the warm water and let stand 5 minutes, or until creamy. In a bowl stir together yeast mixture, 1/3 cup of the water, and 1 cup of the bread flour. Stir 4 minutes, then over bowl with plastic wrap. Let sponge stand at cool room temperature for at least 12 hours and up to 1 day.

2. To Make Bread: In a small bowl stir together yeast and milk and let stand 5 minutes, or until creamy. In bowl of a standing electric mixer fitted with dough hook blend together milk mixture, sponge, water, oil, and flour at low speed until flour is just moistened; add salt and mix until smooth and elastic, about 8 minutes. Scrape dough into an oiled bowl and cover with plastic wrap.

3. Let dough rise at room temperature until doubled in bulk, about 1 1/2 hours. (Dough will be sticky and full of air bubbles.) Turn dough out onto a well-floured work surface and cut in half. Transfer each half to a parchment sheet and form into an irregular oval about 9 inches long. Dimple loaves with floured fingers and dust tops with flour. Cover loaves with a dampened kitchen towel. Let loaves rise at room temperature until almost doubled in bulk, 1 1/2 to 2 hours.

4. At least 45 minutes before baking ciabatta, put a baking stone on oven rack in lowest position in oven and preheat oven to 425 F (220 degrees C).

5. Transfer 1 loaf on its parchment to a rimless baking sheet with a long side of loaf parallel to far edge of baking sheet. Line up far edge of baking sheet with far edge of stone or tiles, and tilt baking sheet to slide loaf with parchment onto back half of stone or tiles. Transfer remaining loaf to front half of stone in a similar manner. Bake ciabatta loaves 20 minutes, or until pale golden. Cool loaves on a wire rack.

Sun-Dried Tomato Focaccia

Yields 8-10 Servings

Ingredients:

- 1 cup water
- 3 cups bread flour
- 2 tablespoons dry milk powder
- 3 1/2 tablespoons white sugar
- 1 teaspoon salt
- 3 tablespoons margarine
- 2 teaspoons active dry yeast
- 1/2 cup chopped sun-dried tomatoes
- 2 tablespoons olive oil
- 2 tablespoons Parmesan cheese
- 2 teaspoons dried rosemary, crushed
- 1 teaspoon garlic salt
- 1 cup shredded mozzarella cheese

Directions:

1. Place water, flour, powdered milk, sugar, salt, butter or margarine, tomatoes, and yeast into bread machine in the order suggested by the manufacturer. Set to Dough cycle, and start the machine. Dough will be 1/2 pound.
2. When the bread machine has finished the Dough cycle, take the dough out. Knead for 1 minute by hand. Place in an oiled bowl, and turn a few times to coat the surface of the dough. Cover with a damp cloth, and let rise for 15 minutes in a warm place.
3. Dust a 10 x 15 inch baking tray with cornmeal. Roll out dough to fit the pan. Make indentations in the dough with your fingertips. Brush top surface with oil, and cover with a damp cloth. Allow to rise for 30 minutes.
4. Sprinkle with parmesan, rosemary, garlic salt, and mozzarella.
5. Bake at 400 degree F (205 degrees C) for 15 minutes, or until nicely browned. Cool slightly, and cut into squares for serving.

Potato and Herb Focaccia

Yields 8-10 Servings

Ingredients:

- 1 tbsp. sugar
- 2 1/2 tsp. (.25-oz) active dry yeast
- 1 1/4 cups water, warm (100-110F)
- 3 – 3 1/2 cups all-purpose flour
- 2 tsp. salt
- 1 tbsp. olive oil

- approx. 1 lb. small potatoes, boiled or steamed, and cooled
- 1/4 cup olive oil
- 3 tbsp. herbs de Provence (or a combination of dried thyme and rosemary)
- 2 tsp. coarse kosher salt or sea salt

Directions:

1. In a large mixing bowl, or the bowl of an electric mixer, combine sugar, yeast and water. Stir mixture and let stand for 5 minutes, until yeast is slightly foamy.
2. Stir in 2 1/2 cups of the flour and the salt – mix with the dough hook of your stand mixer – and dough will start to come together. Gradually stir in the remaining flour until dough pulls away from the sides of the bowl and forms a slightly sticky ball. You may not need all of the remaining flour.
3. Turn out onto a floured surface (or continue to knead with the dough hook for 3-4 minutes) and knead until smooth. Place in a lightly oiled bowl, cover with plastic wrap and let rise until doubled in size, 1 – 1 1/2 hours.
   Preheat oven to 375F.
4. Line a rimmed baking sheet or jelly roll pan (12×18-inches) with parchment paper or grease with olive oil.
5. When dough has risen, punch down the dough gently and turn it out onto prepared pan. Use your fingertips to press and stretch the dough to a rectangle that is roughly 10×16-inches. Brush dough with approx. 3 tbsp. of the olive oil and sprinkle with 2 tbsp. of the Herbs de Provence. Allow dough to rest for 10 minutes.
6. Slice the potatoes into 1/4-inch thick pieces. Arrange on top of the dough and press them down gently. Brush potatoes with remaining olive oil and sprinkle with remaining herbs.
7. Sprinkle coarse salt over the whole focaccia dough.
8. Let the dough rise for 20-30 minutes.
9. Bake bread for 25-30 minutes, or until golden brown.
10. Cool on a wire rack for at least 10 minutes before serving.

Desserts

Ice Cream Base

Yield 8 servings

Ingredients:

- 1 cup heavy cream
- 3 cups half-and-half cream
- 8 egg yolks

- 1 cup white sugar
- 1/8 teaspoon salt
- 1 Teaspoon of vanilla (optional)

Directions:

1. Pour the heavy cream and half-and-half cream into a heavy saucepan, place over medium-low heat, and heat until barely simmering, stirring frequently. Turn the heat down to low.
2. Whisk together the egg yolks, sugar, vanilla (optional) and salt in a large bowl until thoroughly combined.
3. Slowly pour about 1/2 cup of hot cream mixture into the egg yolk mixture, whisking constantly. Repeat three times more, whisking thoroughly before adding each additional 1/2 cup of hot cream to the egg yolk mixture. Pour the egg yolk mixture back into the saucepan with the remaining hot cream, and whisk constantly over medium-low heat until the mixture thickens and will coat the back of a spoon, 5 to 8 minutes. Do not let mixture boil.
4. Pour the ice cream base into a bowl and allow it to cool for about 20 minutes. Place in refrigerator and chill overnight. The next day, pour into an ice cream maker, and freeze according to the manufacturer's directions. Remove the ice cream, pack into a covered container, and freeze for 2 hours or overnight before serving.

You can add any fruit and flavor to the Ice Cream Base to make it your own

Lavender Ice Cream

Yield 12 servings

Ingredients:

- 3 cups milk
- 2 stems of fresh lavender flowers
- 8 egg yolks
- 1 1/2 cups white sugar
- 3 cups heavy cream

Directions:

1. Heat the milk and lavender in a 3-quart saucepan over low heat until warmed through. Remove from heat, and allow lavender to infuse for about 20 minutes. Remove flowers.
2. Beat the egg yolks and sugar together in large bowl.
3. Whisk the lavender-infused milk into the egg mixture, and then pour it back into the saucepan.
4. Heat the mixture over low heat, whisking constantly, until the mixture thickens and can coat the back of a spoon, 7 to 10 minutes. Remove from heat, and cool slightly, about 5 minutes. Stir in the heavy cream. Transfer the mixture to a bowl, and chill in refrigerator at least 4 hours.
5. Pour the chilled mixture into an ice cream maker and freeze according to manufacturer's directions until it reaches "soft-serve" consistency.
6. Transfer ice cream to a lidded container; cover surface with plastic wrap and seal. For best results, ice cream should be place in the freezer at least 2 hours or overnight.

Watermelon Mint Ice Cream

Yield 2 quarts

Ingredients:
- 8 cups watermelon chunks
- 1 cup heavy cream
- 1 cup white sugar
- 2 cups lightly packed fresh mint
- 4 egg yolks
- 1 cup heavy cream

Directions:
1. Puree the watermelon chunks in a blender or food processor until smooth; strain the juices from any remaining solids and set aside, discarding the solids.
2. Heat 1 cup of heavy cream with the sugar in a saucepan over medium-low heat until warmed. Stir the mint leaves to the warmed cream.
3. Cover the saucepan and remove from heat. Allow the mixture to steep at room temperature for 1 hour. Strain into a bowl; discard the mint leaves. Whisk the egg yolks in a bowl until gently beaten.
4. Slowly pour the mint-infused cream into the egg yolks, whisking constantly to prevent cooking the egg; scrape the mixture back into the saucepan and place over medium heat. Stir constantly, scraping the bottom while cooking, until the mixture thickens and coats the spatula; pour the mixture through a strainer into a bowl along with 1 cup heavy cream.
5. Mix the watermelon juice into the cream mixture.
6. Refrigerate overnight for best consistency.
7. Pour into an ice cream maker and freeze according to manufacturer's instructions.

Angel Food Cake

Yield 1 - 10 inch cake

Ingredients:

- 1 1/4 cups cake flour
- 1 3/4 cups white sugar
- 1/4 teaspoon salt
- 1 1/2 cups egg whites
- 1 teaspoon cream of tartar
- 1/2 teaspoon vanilla extract
- 1/2 teaspoon almond extract

Directions:

1. Beat egg whites until they form stiff peaks, and then add cream of tartar, vanilla extract, and almond extract.
2. Sift together flour, sugar, and salt. Repeat five times.
3. Gently combine the egg whites with the dry ingredients, and then pour into an ungreased 10 inch tube pan.
4. Place cake pan in a cold oven. Turn the oven on; set it to 325 degrees F (165 degrees C). Cook for about one hour, or until cake is golden brown.
5. Invert cake, and allow it to cool in the pan. When thoroughly cooled, remove from pan.

Crumb Crust

Yield 1 9-9 ½-inch pie crust

Ingredients:

- 5 tablespoons unsalted butter, melted, use 1 tablespoon for greasing
- 1/8 teaspoon salt
- 1 1/2 cups cookie crumbs (10 graham crackers or 24 small gingersnaps; about 6 oz.)
- 2 tablespoons sugar

Directions:

1. Put oven rack in middle position and preheat oven to 350°F. Lightly butter pie plate.
2. To make cookie crumbs, break up crackers or cookies into small pieces, then pulse in a food processor until finely ground.
3. Stir together all ingredients in a bowl and press evenly on bottom and up side of pie plate.
4. Bake until crisp, 12 to 15 minutes, and then cool on a rack to room temperature, about 45 minutes.

Oatmeal Apple Crisp

Yields 4-6 servings

Ingredients:
- 3-4 c. apples, chopped
- 3 tbsp. flour
- 1/2 c. sugar
- 1/2 tsp. allspice
- 1/2 tsp. nutmeg
- 1 tsp. cinnamon
- 1 1/2 c. brown sugar
- 1 c. oatmeal
- 1 c. flour
- 1/2 c. butter

Directions:
1. Pre heat oven for 375 degrees.
2. Combine apples, white sugar, and brown sugar, 3 tablespoons of flour, cinnamon and nutmeg. Blend well and place in 9"x13" greased baking dish.
3. Combine brown sugar, oatmeal and 1 1/2 cups flour. Into this mixture, cut butter and mix until it becomes crumbly.
4. Spread over the apples. Bake at 375 degrees for about 40 minutes or until apples are tender. Serve hot or cool with cream or ice cream.

Ricotta Cheesecake

Yield 1 - 9 1/2 inch round cheesecake

Ingredients:
- 2 pounds ricotta cheese
- 2/3 cup white sugar
- 1/3 cup all-purpose flour
- 6 eggs
- 1 1/2 cups graham cracker crumbs
- 6 tablespoons butter, melted
- 2 teaspoons orange zest
- 2 teaspoons vanilla extract
- 1/8 teaspoon salt

Directions:
1. Preheat oven to 300 degrees F (150 degrees C). Set rack in the middle of the oven.
2. Combine cookie or graham cracker crumbs with butter or margarine. Press into bottom and partially up sides of 9 inch spring form pan. Refrigerate.
3. Place the ricotta in a large mixing bowl, and stir it as smooth as possible with a rubber spatula. Stir the sugar and flour together thoroughly into the ricotta. Stir in the eggs 1 at a time. Blend in the vanilla, orange zest, and salt. Pour batter into the prepared pan.
4. Bake in the center of the oven for about 1 1/4 to 1 1/2 hours, until a light golden color. Make sure the center is fairly firm, and the point of a sharp knife inserted in the center comes out clean. Cool on a wire rack. It will sink slightly as it cools. Cover, and chill till serving time.

Pumpkin Ginger Cheesecake Pie

Yield 8 servings

Ingredients:

- 1 gingersnap crumb crust baked and cooled
- 3/4 cup sugar
- 1/4 cup chopped crystallized ginger
- 8 ounces cream cheese, softened
- 2 large eggs
- 1/4 cup whole milk
- 1 tablespoon all-purpose flour
- 1/2 teaspoon freshly grated nutmeg
- 1/4 teaspoon salt
- 1 cup canned solid-pack pumpkin (from a 15-ounces can)

Directions:

1. Make gingersnap crumb crust and reserve (see recipe).
2. Put oven rack in middle position and preheat oven to 350°F.
3. Pulse sugar and ginger in a food processor until ginger is finely chopped, then add cream cheese and pulse until smooth. Add eggs, milk, flour, nutmeg, and salt and pulse until just combined.
4. Reserve 2/3 cup cream cheese mixture in a glass measure. Whisk together remaining 1 1/3 cups cream cheese mixture and pumpkin in a large bowl until combined.
5. Pour pumpkin mixture into gingersnap crumb crust. Stir reserved cream cheese mixture (in glass measure) and drizzle decoratively over top of pumpkin mixture, then, if desired, swirl with back of a spoon.
6. Put pie on a baking sheet and bake until center is just set, 35 to 45 minutes. Transfer to a rack and cool to room temperature, about 2 hours, then chill, loosely covered with foil, at least 4 hours. If necessary, very gently blot any moisture from surface with paper towels before serving.

Butter Flaky Pie Crust

Yield 1 single crust pie

Ingredients:
- 1 1/4 cups all-purpose flour
- 1/4 teaspoon salt
- 1/2 cup butter, chilled and diced
- 1/4 cup ice water

Directions:
1. In a large bowl, combine flour and salt. Cut in butter until mixture resembles coarse crumbs. Stir in water, a tablespoon at a time, until mixture forms a ball. Wrap in plastic and refrigerate for 4 hours or overnight.
2. Roll dough out to fit a 9 inch pie plate. Place crust in pie plate. Press the dough evenly into the bottom and sides of the pie plate.
3. For a no baked pie pre-bake the pie crust at 350 degrees for a total of 10-15 minutes or until golden brown.

Pumpkin Pie

Yield 1 - 9 inch pie

Ingredients:
- 1 recipe pastry for a 9 inch single crust pie
- 3 eggs
- 1 egg yolk
- 1/2 cup white sugar
- 1/2 cup packed brown sugar
- 1 teaspoon salt
- 1/2 teaspoon ground cinnamon
- 1/2 teaspoon ground nutmeg
- 1/2 teaspoon ground ginger
- 1/4 teaspoon ground cloves
- 1 1/2 cups milk
- 1/2 cup heavy whipping cream
- 2 cups pumpkin puree

Directions:
1. Preheat oven to 425 degrees F (220 degrees C.)
2. In a large bowl, combine eggs, egg yolk, white sugar and brown sugar. Add salt, cinnamon, nutmeg, ginger and cloves. Gradually stir in milk and cream. Stir in pumpkin. Pour filling into pie shell.
3. Bake for ten minutes in preheated oven. Reduce heat to 350 degrees F (175 degrees C), and bake for an additional 40 to 45 minutes or until filling is set.

Chocolate Chip Bread Pudding with Walnuts

Yield 6 servings

Ingredients:

- 4 cups 1-inch Day old crusty bread (about 6 ounces)
- 1 1/4 cups semisweet or bittersweet chocolate chips, divided
- 1/2 cup walnuts, toasted, broken into 1/2-inch pieces (optional)
- 1 cup heavy whipping cream, divided
- 1 cup half and half, divided
- 5 tablespoons unsweetened cocoa powder
- 4 large eggs
- 1 large egg yolk
- 1/2 cup sugar

Directions:

1. Toss bread cubes, 1/2 cup chocolate chips, and toasted walnuts in large bowl to blend.
2. Whisk 1/2 cup cream, 1/2 cup half and half, and cocoa in heavy medium saucepan to blend. Add remaining 3/4 cup chocolate chips; stir over low heat until melted and smooth.
3. Gradually whisk in remaining 1/2 cup cream and 1/2 cup half and half. Whisk eggs, egg yolk, and sugar in medium bowl to blend. Whisk in chocolate-cream mixture. Stir into bread mixture. Let stand 1 hour for bread to absorb some of custard.
4. Preheat oven to 325°F. Butter six (1- to 1 1/4-cup) ramekins. Divide pudding mixture among ramekins. Bake puddings until set in centers, about 40 minutes.

*Top warm puddings with whipped cream and serve. *

Pumpkin Flan

Yield 8 servings

Ingredients:

For caramel and flan:
- 2 cups sugar
- 1 1/2 cups heavy cream
- 1 cup whole milk
- 5 whole large eggs plus 1 large egg yolk
- 1 (15-ounce) can solid-pack pumpkin (1 3/4 cups; not pie filling)

- 1 teaspoon vanilla
- 1 1/2 teaspoons ground cinnamon
- 1 teaspoon ground ginger
- 1/4 teaspoon ground nutmeg
- 1/4 teaspoon salt

Directions:

Make caramel:
1. Put oven rack in middle position and preheat oven to 350°F. Heat soufflé dish in oven while making caramel.
2. Cook 1 cup sugar in a dry 2-quart heavy saucepan over moderate heat, undisturbed, until it begins to melt. Continue to cook, stirring occasionally with a fork, until sugar melts into a deep golden caramel.
3. Wearing oven mitts remove hot dish from oven and immediately pour caramel into dish, tilting it to cover bottom and side. (Leave oven on.) Keep tilting as caramel cools and thickens enough to coat, then let harden.

Make flan:
1. Bring cream and milk to a bare simmer in a 2-quart heavy saucepan over moderate heat, and then remove from heat.
2. Whisk together whole eggs, yolk, and remaining cup sugar in a large bowl until combined well, then whisk in pumpkin, vanilla, spices, and salt until combined well. Add hot cream mixture in a slow stream, whisking. Pour custard through a fine-mesh sieve into a bowl, scraping with a rubber spatula to force through, and stir to combine well.
3. Pour custard over caramel in dish, and then bake in a water bath until flan is golden brown on top and a knife inserted in center comes out clean, about 1 1/4 hours.
4. Remove dish from water bath and transfer to a rack to cool. Chill flan, covered, until cold, at least 6 hours.

To serve:

Run a thin knife between flan and side of dish to loosen. Shake dish gently from side to side and, when flan moves freely in dish, invert a large platter with a lip over dish. Holding dish and platter securely together, quickly invert and turn out flan onto platter. (Caramel will pour out over and around flan.)

Vanilla Crème Brûlée with Raspberries

Yield 6 servings

Ingredients:

- 6 tablespoons raspberry jam
- 2 1/2-pint baskets fresh raspberries
- 6 large egg yolks
- 6 tablespoons sugar
- 1 vanilla bean, split lengthwise
- 1 1/2 cups whipping cream
- 12 teaspoons (packed) golden brown sugar

Directions:

1. Preheat oven to 325°F. Spread 1 tablespoon jam over bottom of each of six 3/4-cup soufflé dishes or custard cups. Press 7 berries, placed on their sides, into jam in each dish. Reserve remaining raspberries for garnish.
2. Whisk yolks and 6 tablespoons sugar in medium bowl to blend. Scrape in seeds from vanilla bean. Gradually whisk in cream. Divide mixture among dishes. Arrange dishes in 13x9x2-inch baking pan. Pour enough hot water into pan to come halfway up sides of dishes.
3. Bake custards until set in center, about 40 minutes. Place pan on work surface. Cool custards in water 30 minutes. Remove from water; chill overnight.
4. Preheat broiler. Sprinkle 2 teaspoons of brown sugar on top of each custard. Place dishes on small baking sheet. Broil until sugar just starts to caramelize, rotating sheet for even browning, about 2 minutes. Chill until topping hardens, about 2 hours. Garnish with reserved berries.

Cookies

Anginetti Cookies
Italian Cookies

Yield 2 Dozen

Ingredients:
- 1/2 cup white sugar
- 6 tablespoons butter
- 2 teaspoons vanilla extract
- 1 teaspoon lemon zest
- 3 eggs
- 2 cups all-purpose flour
- 2 teaspoons baking powder
- 1 tablespoon butter
- 3 cups sifted confectioners' sugar
- 2 tablespoons water
- 2 tablespoons lemon juice
- 1 teaspoon vanilla extract

Directions:
1. Preheat oven to 350 degrees F. Line cookie sheet with parchment paper.
2. In a mixing bowl beat sugar, vanilla, lemon zest and 6 tablespoons of butter with an electric mixer until well blended. Add eggs one at a time, beating well after each addition. Continue to beat for 1 minute.
3. Stir in flour and baking powder (dough be soft and sticky). Spoon dough into a pastry bag fitted with a 3/8-inch round tip. Pipe 2-inch diameter rings onto the prepared cookie sheet.
4. With moistened fingertips, press ends of each ring together to form a smooth ring.
5. Bake about 20 minutes or until golden brown.
6. To make icing: Melt 1 tablespoon of butter over low heat. Add sugar, water, lemon juice and vanilla and whisk until sugar melts and mixture is heated through. Thin with more water if icing is too thick to brush. For colored icing use a few drops of food coloring in the icing mixture
7. Remove cookies from oven and immediately brush warm icing over hot cookies. Cool iced cookies on sheet for 2 minutes. Transfer to a rack and cool completely.

Chocolate Chip Cookies

Yield 4 dozen

Ingredients:

- 1 cup butter, softened
- 1 cup white sugar
- 1 cup packed brown sugar
- 2 eggs
- 2 teaspoons vanilla extract
- 3 cups all-purpose flour
- 1 teaspoon baking soda
- 2 teaspoons hot water
- 1/2 teaspoon salt
- 2 cups semisweet chocolate chips
- 1 cup chopped walnuts

Directions:

1. Preheat oven to 350 degrees F (175 degrees C).
2. Cream together the butter, white sugar, and brown sugar until smooth. Beat in the eggs one at a time, then stir in the vanilla. Dissolve baking soda in hot water. Add to batter along with salt. Stir in flour, chocolate chips, and nuts. Drop by large spoonful's onto ungreased pans.
3. Bake for about 10 minutes in the preheated oven, or until edges are nicely browned.

Easy Sugar Cookies

Yield 4 dozen

Ingredients:

- 2 3/4 cups all-purpose flour
- 1 teaspoon baking soda
- 1/2 teaspoon baking powder
- 1 cup butter, softened
- 1 1/2 cups white sugar
- 1 egg
- 1 teaspoon vanilla extract

Directions:

1. Preheat oven to 375 degrees F (190 degrees C). In a small bowl, stir together flour, baking soda, and baking powder. Set aside.
2. In a large bowl, cream together the butter and sugar until smooth. Beat in egg and vanilla. Gradually blend in the dry ingredients.
3. Roll rounded teaspoonful of dough into balls, and place onto ungreased cookie sheets.
4. Bake 8 to 10 minutes in the preheated oven, or until golden. Let stand on cookie sheet two minutes before removing to cool on wire racks.

Lemon Rosemary Cookies

Yield 6 dozen

Ingredients:

- 1/2 cup butter, softened
- 1/2 cup sugar
- 1 tablespoon lemon zest
- 1/2 teaspoon fresh rosemary
- 1 egg

- 1 1/2 cups all-purpose flour
- 1/4 teaspoon baking soda
- 1/8 teaspoon salt
- 3 tablespoons sugar
- 1 teaspoon lemon zest

Directions:

1. In large bowl, beat butter, 1/2 cup sugar, 1 tablespoon lemon zest, the rosemary and egg with electric mixer on medium speed, or mix with spoon. Stir in flour, baking soda and salt.
2. Divide dough in half. Shape each half into 9-inch roll, 3/4 to 1 inch in diameter. Wrap and refrigerate about 2 hours or until firm.
3. Preheat oven to 375 degrees. Mix 3 tablespoons sugar and 1 teaspoon lemon zest. Roll dough in sugar mixture to coat. Cut rolls into 1/4-inch slices. Place about 2 inches apart on ungreased cookie sheet. Bake 5 to 8 minutes or until edges are light brown. Immediately remove from cookie sheet to wire rack. Cool completely.

Orange Cranberry Drops

Yield 3 dozen

Ingredients:
- 1/2 cup white sugar
- 1/2 cup packed brown sugar
- 1/4 cup butter, softened
- 1 egg
- 3 tablespoons orange juice
- 1/2 teaspoon orange extract
- 2 teaspoon grated orange zest
- 1 1/2 cups all-purpose flour
- 1/2 teaspoon baking powder
- 1/4 teaspoon baking soda
- 1/4 teaspoon salt
- 1 cup dried cranberries

Directions:
1. Preheat oven to 375 degrees F (190 degrees C). Lightly grease cookie sheets, or line with parchment paper.
2. In a medium bowl, cream together the white sugar, brown sugar, and butter. Stir in the egg, orange juice, orange extract, and orange zest. Sift together the flour, baking powder, baking soda, and salt; mix into the orange mixture. Stir in the dried cranberries.
3. Drop cookie dough by heaping teaspoonful, 2 inches apart, on the prepared cookie sheets.
4. Bake for 10 to 12 minutes, or until edges are starting to brown. Cool on baking sheets for 5 minutes, and then remove to a wire rack to cool completely.

Peanut Butter Cookies

Yield 4 dozen

Ingredients:
- 1 cup unsalted butter
- 1 cup crunchy peanut butter
- 1 cup white sugar
- 1 cup packed brown sugar
- 2 eggs
- 2 1/2 cups all-purpose flour
- 1 teaspoon baking powder
- 1/2 teaspoon salt
- 1 1/2 teaspoons baking soda

Directions:
1. Cream together butter, peanut butter and sugars. Beat in eggs.
2. In a separate bowl, sift together flour, baking powder, baking soda, and salt. Stir into batter. Put batter in refrigerator for 1 hour.
3. Roll into 1 inch balls and put on baking sheets. Flatten each ball with a fork, making a crisscross pattern.
4. Bake in a preheated 375 degrees F oven for about 10 minutes or until cookies begin to brown. Do not over-bake.

Peppermint Meringue Cookies

Yield 56 cookies

Ingredients:
- 2 egg whites
- 1/8 teaspoon cider vinegar
- 1/8 teaspoon salt
- 1/3 cup white sugar
- 3 peppermint candy canes, crushed

Directions:
1. Preheat the oven to 225 degrees F (110 degrees C). Line cookie sheets with aluminum foil or parchment paper.
2. In a large glass or metal bowl, whip egg whites, vinegar and salt to soft peaks. Gradually add sugar while continuing to whip until stiff peaks form, about 5 minutes. Fold in 1/3 of the crushed candy canes, reserving the rest.
3. Drop by heaping teaspoonful, one inch apart onto the prepared cookie sheets. Sprinkle remaining crushed candy canes over the top.
4. Bake for 90 minutes in the preheated oven, or until dry. Cool on baking sheets.

Peppermint Snickerdoodles

Yields 4 dozen

Ingredients:
- 2 cups sugar
- 2 tsp. ground cinnamon
- 1/2 cup finely chopped peppermints or candy canes
- 1 cup butter, soft
- 2 large eggs

- 1 1/2 tsp. vanilla extract
- 2 3/4 cups all-purpose flour
- 1/4 tsp. salt
- 2 tsp. cream of tartar
- 1 tsp. baking soda

Directions:
1. Preheat the oven to 375F. Line a baking sheet with parchment paper.
2. Place 1/2 cup of the sugar in a shallow dish or bowl and whisk cinnamon to combine with it. Add in chopped peppermints. Set aside.
3. In a large bowl, cream together the butter and remaining sugar (1 1/2 cups sugar) until fluffy. Beat in eggs, one at a time, and the vanilla extract.
4. In a medium bowl, whisk together flour, salt, cream of tartar and baking soda. Add to butter mixture and stir until fully incorporated.
5. Shape dough into 1 inch balls and roll in the peppermint sugar mixture.
6. Place on baking sheet, leaving 2 inches between balls to allow for spreading.
7. Bake for about 9-11 minutes, until cookies are set and edges are very lightly browned.
8. Cool for 3-4 minutes on the baking sheet, and then transfer cookies to a wire rack to cool completely.

Vanilla Madeleines

Yields 2 dozen

Ingredients:

- 2 large eggs, room temperature
- 2/3 cup sugar*
- 2 tsp. vanilla extract
- 8 tbsp. butter, melted and cooled
- 1/8 tsp. salt
- 1 cup all-purpose flour
- 1/4 tsp. baking powder

Directions:

1. Preheat oven to 375F. Lightly grease and flour your madeleine pans (unless you are using nonstick, in which case light greasing is all that is necessary).
2. In a large bowl, beat together eggs and sugar until smooth and thick, 1-2 minutes. Add in vanilla and salt. Sift flour and baking powder into the bowl and mix until it is just combined, and no streaks of flour remain visible.
3. Slowly add in the melted butter, streaming it in while you stir constantly (or mix at a low speed) and it is well combined.
4. Place a generous 1 tbsp. batter into each cavity of your prepared pan.
5. Bake for 12-14 minutes, until cookies are golden around the edges.
6. Allow to cool for 3-5 minutes before removing from the pan. The pan should be cooled, regressed and floured before filling it with more batter (it is ok if the batter must be used in batches) for another batch.

Sage-Scented Shortbread

Yield 32 cookies

Ingredients:
- 2 cups all-purpose flour
- 1/2 cup powdered sugar
- 2 tablespoons thinly sliced fresh sage leaves or 2 teaspoons dried sage
- 1 teaspoon coarse kosher salt
- 1 cup (2 sticks) unsalted butter, cut into 1/2-inch-thick pieces, room temperature

Directions:
1. Blend first 4 ingredients in processor. Add butter; using on/off turns, process until dough comes together.
2. Divide in half. Shape each dough piece into log about 1 1/2 inches in diameter. Chill until firm enough to slice, about 30 minutes.
3. Position 1 rack in top third and 1 rack in bottom third of oven; preheat to 350°F. Line 2 baking sheets with parchment. Cut each dough log into 1/3- to 1/2-inch-thick rounds; place on sheets.
4. Bake 10 minutes. Reverse sheets so bottom sheet is on top rack of oven and top sheet is on bottom rack. Bake until cookies are golden, about 15 minutes longer. Cool on racks.

Whoopie Pies

Makes 8 individual desserts

Ingredients:

For cakes:
- 2 cups all-purpose flour
- 1/2 cup Dutch-process cocoa powder
- 1 1/4 teaspoons baking soda
- 1 teaspoon salt
- 1 cup well-shaken buttermilk
- 1 teaspoon vanilla
- 1 stick (1/2 cup) unsalted butter, softened
- 1 cup packed brown sugar
- 1 large egg

For filling:
- 1 stick (1/2 cup) unsalted butter, softened or 1/2 cup of vegetable shortening
- 1 1/4 cups confectionary sugar
- 2 cups marshmallow cream such or Marshmallow Fluff
- 1 teaspoon vanilla

Directions:

Make cakes:
Preheat oven to 350°F.
1. Whisk together flour, cocoa, baking soda, and salt in a bowl until combined. Stir together buttermilk and vanilla in a small bowl.
2. Beat together butter and brown sugar in a large bowl with an electric mixer at medium-high speed until pale and fluffy, about 3 minutes in a standing mixer or 5 minutes with a handheld, then add egg, beating until combined well. Reduce speed to low and alternately mix in flour mixture and buttermilk in batches, beginning and ending with flour, scraping down side of bowl occasionally, and mixing until smooth.
3. Spoon 1/4-cup mounds of batter about 2 inches apart onto 2 buttered large baking sheets. Bake in upper and lower thirds of oven, switching position of sheets halfway through baking, until tops are puffed and cakes spring back when touched, 11 to 13 minutes. Transfer with a metal spatula to a rack to cool completely.

Make filling:
1. Beat together butter, confectionary sugar, marshmallow, and vanilla in a bowl with electric mixer at medium speed until smooth, about 3 minutes.

Whoopie Pies (Cont.)

Assemble pies:
1. Spread a rounded tablespoon filling on flat sides of half of cakes and top with remaining cakes.

   Cooks' notes: Cakes can be made 3 days ahead and kept, layered between sheets of wax paper, in an airtight container at room temperature.

   Filling can be made 4 hours ahead and kept, covered, at room temperature.

   *If you are allergic to gelatin then use marshmallow cream

This

&

That

Jamaican Jerk Rub

Yield 3 Tablespoons

Ingredients:

- 1 1/2 teaspoons ground allspice
- 1 1/2 teaspoons dried thyme
- 1 teaspoon curry powder
- 1 1/2 teaspoons paprika
- 1 teaspoon brown sugar
- 1/2 teaspoon salt
- 3/4 teaspoon black pepper
- 2 teaspoons cayenne pepper
- 1/4 teaspoon grated nutmeg
- 1/4 teaspoon ground cinnamon
- 1/8 teaspoon ground cloves
- 1 teaspoon of turmeric

Directions:

1. Mix together all spices thoroughly and store in an airtight container.
2. To use, rub on chicken, pork, or fish 15-20 minutes before grilling or overnight for a fuller flavor.
3. This recipe should do about 3 pounds of meat.

Apple Butter Barbeque Sauce

Yield 3 cups

Ingredients:

- 11/2 cup Apple Butter
- 1/2 cup ketchup
- 2 cups unpacked brown sugar
- 6 tablespoons lemon juice
- 1/2 teaspoon salt
- 1/2 teaspoon ground black pepper
- 1/2 teaspoon paprika
- 1/2 teaspoon garlic powder
- 1/2 teaspoon ground cinnamon

Directions:

1. In a saucepan over medium heat, mix Apple butter, ketchup, brown sugar, lemon juice, salt, pepper, paprika, garlic powder, and cinnamon. Bring mixture to a boil. Remove from heat, and cool completely. Use to baste the meat of your choice.

I like to use this on my apple butter glazed smoked pork shoulder

Tip of the day

- Did you know that you can substitute 1 tsp. Allspice for 1/2 tsp. cinnamon + 1/2 tsp. ground cloves

- Did you know that you can substitute 1 tsp. Apple Pie Spice for 1/2 tsp. cinnamon, 1/4 tsp. nutmeg, 1/8 tsp. cardamom

- Whenever possible, warm your dinner plates slightly in the oven before serving so the meal stays a little bit hotter.

- Buy several small spray bottles to use in the kitchen, for tasks like moistening pie dough, coating oil on pans, misting salad dressing on delicate greens, or other purposes you might think of.

- Don't waste pie pastry scraps ... sprinkle with cinnamon and sugar, and bake like cookies.

- Did you know that you can make the cookie dough ahead of time, and freeze it for later use? All you need to do is make the dough, place parchment paper on a cookie sheet and form the dough in balls like the recipe says to do then place the cookie sheet in the freezer overnight. I then remove the cookies from the sheet pan and put them in Ziploc baggies label and date them. They will keep for up to 1 year. Then you can use them for later use.

- Store spices in a cool, dark place. Humidity, light and heat will cause herbs and spices to lose their flavor more quickly. Although the most convenient place for your spice rack may be above your stove, moving your spices to a different location may keep them fresh longer.

- Freeze seasonal fruit to enjoy all year long. Leave berries and pitted cherries whole, but slice melons and stone fruit into wedges. Spread in a single layer on a parchment-paper-lined baking sheet, sprinkle with sugar and freeze until solid. Transfer to a freezer bag and freeze for up to 1 year.